D0009177

920
MASTERS   Masters of music.

$478.80   3254716014915

Masters of Music

THE WORLD'S GREATEST COMPOSERS

The Life and Times of

John Philip Sousa

Mitchell Lane
PUBLISHERS

P.O. Box 196
Hockessin, Delaware 19707

Masters of Music
THE WORLD'S GREATEST COMPOSERS

Titles in the Series
The Life and Times of...

Johann Sebastian Bach

Ludwig van Beethoven

Irving Berlin

Hector Berlioz

Leonard Bernstein

Johannes Brahms

Frederic Chopin

Duke Ellington

Stephen Foster

Kenny G.

George Gershwin

George Frideric Handel

Franz Joseph Haydn

Scott Joplin

Franz Liszt

Felix Mendelssohn

Wolfgang Amadeus Mozart

Franz Peter Schubert

John Philip Sousa

Igor Stravinsky

Peter Ilyich Tchaikovsky

Giuseppe Verdi

Antonio Lucio Vivaldi

Richard Wagner

Visit us on the web: www.mitchelllane.com
Comments? email us: mitchelllane@mitchelllane.com

Masters of Music

THE WORLD'S GREATEST COMPOSERS

The Life and Times of

John Philip Sousa

by Susan Zannos

Printing   2   3   4   5   6   7   8

          Library of Congress Cataloging-in-Publication Data
Zannos, Susan.
          The Life and Times of John Philip Sousa / Susan Zannos.
                    p. cm. — (Masters of music. The world's greatest composers)
          Summary: A biography of the famous band leader and composer who was known as the
          March King. Includes sidebars on such topics as ragtime music, the Civil War, and
          trapshooting.
          Includes bibliographical references (p.) and index.
                    ISBN 1-58415-212-5 (lib bdg.)
          1. Sousa, John Philip, 1854-1932—Juvenile literature. 2. Composers—United States—
          Biography—Juvenile literature. [1. Sousa, John Philip, 1854-1932. 2. Composers. 3. Musi-
          cians.] I. Title. II. Series.
          ML3930.S7Z26 2003
          784.8'4'092—dc21   2003000351

ABOUT THE AUTHOR: Susan Zannos has been a lifelong educator, having taught at all levels, from preschool to college, in Mexico, Greece, Italy, Russia, and Lithuania, as well as in the United States. She has published a mystery *Trust the Liar* (Walker and Co.) and *Human Types: Essence and the Enneagram* (Samuel Weiser). Her book, *Human Types*, was recently translated into Russian, and in 2003 Susan was invited to tour Russia and lecture about her book. Another book she wrote for young adults, *Careers in Education* (Mitchell Lane) was selected for the New York Public Library's "Books for the Teen Age 2003 List." She has written many books for children, including *Chester Carlson and the Development of Xerography* and *The Life and Times of Ludwig van Beethoven* (Mitchell Lane). Her great interest in composers inspired her to write this book. When not traveling, Susan lives in the Sierra Foothills of Northern California.

Contents

The Life and Times of
John Philip Sousa
by Susan Zannos

* For Your Information

John Philip Sousa, the legendary leader of "The President's Own" U.S. Marine Band, wears the impressive official uniform of leader of the U.S. Marine Band in this undated painting from the U.S. Marines. Sousa was the 17th director of the band which is now more than 200 years old.

The Young Marine

It was a warm spring afternoon in 1868. Young John Philip Sousa was playing his violin in his Washington, D.C. home. Suddenly, according to Sousa's autobiography, *Marching Along*, he was interrupted by a knock at the door.

He didn't recognize the man standing politely on the front porch.

"Good afternoon, young man," said the stranger. "I overheard your wonderful playing."

"Thank you," John Philip said.

"I'm the leader of the circus band that's in town," the man continued. "I think that you play as well as anyone in my group."

The boy knew he was a good musician. It was flattering that this stranger thought so too.

But he was staggered by what the man said next.

"We're striking our tents and leaving town early tomorrow morning," he continued. "I'd like you to come along with us."

John Philip thought quickly. Circus life would be exciting. And someday he might even become the leader of the band.

But there was one problem.

"My father would never let me go," he said.

The man smiled. "Don't tell him. Just sneak out of the house. And be sure to bring your violin."

After telling the youngster where he should go to meet the circus, the man said goodbye and walked away. John Philip could barely restrain his excitement. He was going to play in the circus band!

Inevitably, however, John Philip had to tell someone his secret. He was so excited! He decided to tell his next-door-neighbor, Edward Accardi, and he pledged him to secrecy. Ed, however, immediately told his mother of John Philip's good fortune. Ed's mother told John Philip's mother.

John Philip was dreaming of circus triumphs, of conducting a gigantic band underneath a circus tent, when he felt a hand on his shoulder.

"Wake up, son," said his father, Antonio.

John Philip rubbed the sleep from his eyes. Firmly, his father told him to get dressed in his best Sunday clothes.

Then Antonio and John Philip left the house. A few minutes later, they arrived at the headquarters of the U.S. Marine Corps. It was a place with which Antonio was very familiar, as he was a trombonist in the U.S. Marine Band.

This is a typical circus band that Sousa dreamed of joining in the late 1800s. According to Sousa, he had visions of ladies in spangled tights and of pink lemonade in buckets. He told his friend Ed about his invitation to join the circus. Though Sousa pledged Ed to secrecy, Ed told his mother, who in turn told Sousa's mother. The next day, Sousa's parents foiled his plot to join the circus.

His parents had discovered the plot. It was obvious that young John Philip was a very ambitious boy. Antonio didn't have any objections to his son having a musical career. He just wanted to have more control over it.

So he had contacted the Marine Corps commandant. Together, the two men quickly worked out their own plan.

John Philip Sousa's teenage years were quite unusual as he became an enlisted marine at the age of thirteen. This perchance enlistment led to a lifetime of dedication to the U.S. Marine Corps Band. Here he is shown with members of the Marine Band in 1890.

The result was that early on the morning of June 9, 1868, John Philip Sousa became a member of the United States Marine Corps.

He was 13 years old. ◆

Gilbert and Sullivan FYInfo

Three years after young John Philip Sousa became a Marine, William Gilbert and Arthur Sullivan began one of the most successful and famous musical collaborations in history. While both men had achieved some success before their meeting, it was what they did together that made them immortal.

Gilbert was born in London in 1836. From an early age he was known for his wit and sarcasm. By the time he was 25 years old he was writing humorous verse for the British magazine *Fun*. Soon afterward, he began writing plays. In 1871, seven of his plays had their premieres.

Sullivan was born in London in 1842. His musical ability was obvious from a very young age. His father was bandmaster at the Royal Military College, and by the time the boy was eight years old he could play most of the instruments in the band. He studied at the Royal Academy of Music and the Leipzig Conservatory. Then he began a career as a composer of classical music.

The two men were introduced in 1871. Their first joint operetta, *Thespis*, enjoyed a modest success. Four years later they joined forces with promoter Richard D'Oyly Carte. In the next 15 years, they produced 11 operettas. All were incredibly popular.

The talents of the two men were perfectly suited to each other. Gilbert's satirical words were perfectly set to music by Sullivan's lilting scores. Together they produced music that made people laugh and made them sing. The songs from Gilbert and Sullivan shows like *H.M.S. Pinafore*, *Pirates of Penzance* and *The Mikado* were popular not only in England but in America as well. Touring companies performed Gilbert and Sullivan operettas in every small town. And, as a result of their firm artistic controls, their shows frequently ran for hundreds of performances wherever they were produced.

But they had several differences which caused a split in 1890. They got back together and produced two more operettas, though neither was up to the standards of the ones that had gone before. Their final parting came in 1896.

Sullivan died four years later, while Gilbert lived until 1911. Today, dozens of Gilbert and Sullivan societies throughout the world still regularly perform their works.

This is the house in Washington, DC where John Philip Sousa was born. It is a landmark in the southeastern section. It stands at 636 G Street in a section of town then known as the "Navy Yard." The home was one and a half blocks west of the Marine Barracks. The Sousas moved here early in 1854. In the early part of 1855, the Sousas moved one block farther west on G Street. In 1858, Antonio built a larger house on the southeast corner of Seventh and E Streets, SE. This house became home for the rest of their lives.

CHAPTER 2

An All-American Boy

J ohn Philip Sousa was born in Washington D.C., on November 6, 1854. Antonio Sousa, John Philip's father, was Portuguese. He came to the United States sometime during the 1840s and soon entered the U.S. Navy as a musician. While he was stationed in Brooklyn, Antonio met Marie Elisabeth Trinkaus. She was a young woman from Bavaria (part of modern-day Germany) who was visiting relatives. The two were married in 1849. Their first child, a daughter named Catherine, was born in 1850. A second daughter died before John Philip was born.

The family moved to Washington early in 1854 when Antonio enlisted in the United States Marines as a trombone player in the Marine Band. Four years later he purchased a corner lot and built a larger home for his family. John Philip, his older sister Catherine, and the four younger children who survived grew up in that comfortable house.

From his earliest years, John Philip Sousa had a strong will. He was determined to have his own way. When he was five years old, he became angry with his mother because she would not allow him to have as many doughnuts as he wanted. To teach her a lesson he went out into a cold rain and made a bench out of a plank laid across two trestles. He lay on the bench in the rain for half an hour before his mother found him. By that time he was soaked and chilled. The result of this odd tantrum was a serious case of pneumonia that ruined his health for over a year.

His long illness meant that he couldn't begin school. His mother and father and sister Catherine taught John Philip to read and write. So he was well-prepared when he started school at a little private school across the street from his home. Then he went to a larger one down the block. After that he applied to the public primary school in the district, but quickly transferred to a more advanced school.

By then, the Civil War was raging. Despite its horrors, the conflict pointed John Philip toward his future career. Washington D.C. was filled with military bands. He quickly realized that he wanted to be a musician. In his autobiography he wrote, "I have no recollection of any real desire ever to be anything else. Washington was, in those Civil War days, an armed camp, and there were bands galore. Strange is the boy who doesn't love a band!"

In spite of his love for music, his first music lessons were not a success. His teacher was an elderly man with a short temper, which only provoked John Philip's stubbornness. One evening when the teacher came to the Sousas' house, he realized he had lost his glasses. John Philip and his family went out with candles to look for them. The boy found them and slipped them into his pocket without telling the others. He let the search go on until it was far too late for his music lesson. Then, when they all returned to the house, he slipped the glasses into the pocket of the teacher's coat. John Philip went off to bed, leaving his door open so he could hear the surprised voices when his teacher put on his coat and found the glasses.

Soon after the episode of the lost glasses, the old teacher's son, John Esputa Jr., opened an evening conservatory of music in his home. The school was only a block away from the Sousa home. Even though Esputa had his father's bad temper, he was an excellent musician and John Philip received a good grounding in music. Esputa soon realized that the boy was extremely gifted. He was able to read music and had perfect pitch.

When examinations were held after the third year, John Philip won all of the medals. Shortly afterwards the boy and his teacher had a violent argument. John Philip went home in a rage. He said he didn't want to study music. Instead he planned to be a baker. Antonio Sousa didn't argue with his son. He arranged for the boy to work with a local baker at night. He insisted, however, that his son continue going to school during the day.

This is a photograph of John Philip and his mother, Maria Elisabeth, later in life. Both his mother and father were immigrants. His father was born in Spain of Portuguese parentage, and his mother was born in Bavaria. Both were of middle class families; however, several accounts say his father was descended of nobility.

The first night at the bakery went well. John Philip worked all night and helped load the wagon and deliver the bread in the morning. Then he went home, had his breakfast, and went to school. The second night was less enjoyable, and by the third night it seemed to the boy that the baker was a terrible tyrant. When he got home and his father asked him how he felt, he fell asleep in his chair before he could answer. Later, when his father asked him if he still wanted to be a baker, he said that he'd rather die than be a baker.

At this point Antonio Sousa suggested that his son should make up with his music teacher. In his autobiography Sousa said, "Thus it was that my father brought Professor Esputa and myself together again and we buried the hatchet for good...To prove my sincerity, I studied hard and made great progress in orchestration, harmony, and sight-reading."

During his four years in Esputa's school, John Philip studied voice, violin, piano, flute, cornet, baritone, trombone and alto horn. He had difficulty with the trombone, so his father gave him private lessons at home. When they had spare time, Antonio Sousa took John Philip hunting and fishing. The boy also liked competitive sports like baseball and boxing.

When young Sousa was eleven years old, he formed a dance band composed of seven grown men and himself. The little orchestra performed at dances organized by a man who ran a dance academy. Unfortunately the men convinced John Philip that he should ask their sponsor for more money. When he did, he was fired. The others continued playing for the same wages.

Two years later the circus bandleader appeared on his front porch. One of the most illustrious careers in U.S. musical history was about to begin. ◆

THE CIVIL WAR

Abraham Lincoln, who opposed slavery, was elected president in November, 1860. Southern slave owners were afraid that Lincoln would force them to free their slaves. On December 20, 1860 South Carolina seceded from the United States of America. Mississippi, Florida, Alabama, Georgia, Louisiana, and Texas all followed within two months. They formed the Confederate States of America on February 9. Jefferson Davis was named president.

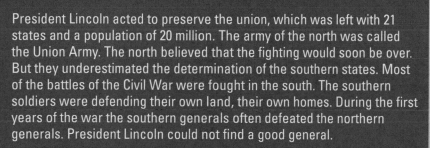

After the opening shots of the Civil War were fired on April 12, 1861, Virginia, Arkansas, Tennessee and North Carolina joined the Confederacy. The eleven states had a combined population of nine million people. Four million of those were slaves.

President Lincoln acted to preserve the union, which was left with 21 states and a population of 20 million. The army of the north was called the Union Army. The north believed that the fighting would soon be over. But they underestimated the determination of the southern states. Most of the battles of the Civil War were fought in the south. The southern soldiers were defending their own land, their own homes. During the first years of the war the southern generals often defeated the northern generals. President Lincoln could not find a good general.

On January 1, 1863, Lincoln issued the Emancipation Proclamation, freeing the slaves in the rebel states. Five months later the brilliant Southern general Robert E. Lee took the battle onto northern soil as he crossed into Pennsylvania. But he was defeated at the Battle of Gettysburg on July 1-3. Meanwhile Union General Ulysses S. Grant lay siege to Vicksburg, Mississippi. When the city surrendered, Grant gained control of the Mississippi River. This cut the Confederacy in half. Lincoln had finally found the general he had been praying for.

In March, 1864 General Grant was promoted to commander of the Union Army. The Union soldiers passed through many of the southern states, living off the land and destroying everything in their path.

President Lincoln was reelected in November. On April 2, 1865 Richmond, the capital of the Confederacy, fell. On April 9, General Lee surrendered to General Grant at Appomattox Court House, ending the Civil War. Five days later President Lincoln was assassinated.

The military engagements of the Civil War resulted in over one million total casualties. The South was left in ruins, the countryside lay in waste, and buildings and bridges were destroyed.

This photograph was made of John Philip between the ages of 19 and 21. The autographed version of this original photograph contains conflicting dates. At the age of 21, Sousa settled in Philadelphia for four years, after having traveled as an orchestra leader with two theater companies.

The March King

John Philip Sousa spent his teen-age years with the Marine Band. During the day he was a Marine and a band musician. In his off-duty hours in the evenings he played professionally at every chance he had. One of these was in an orchestra conducted by George Benkert, who was also a music teacher. Sousa took private lessons from him. Benkert gently encouraged the young Sousa in his compositions, a welcome change from the harsh criticism he'd received from Esputa.

At one point Sousa asked Benkert, an outstanding pianist, for piano lessons. But Benkert refused. In his autobiography, *Marching Along*, Sousa explained that Benkert told him that if he played the piano he would probably use it to compose, and his fingers would "fall into pleasant places where somebody else's have fallen before." Sousa's later career as one of the most original composers in America proved his teacher's wisdom.

When Sousa was nearly 19, Louis Schneider became the leader of the Marine Band. John Philip composed a march, "Salutation," to honor the new director. The band was playing the march on the parade field as Schneider approached. When he learned that a young band member had written it, Schneider ordered the music put away. After that incident the young composer had no use for Schneider. He soon got a special discharge from the Marine Corps.

After leaving the Marines, young Sousa found a series of jobs in theater orchestras as both conductor and violinist.

He also found himself falling in love.

Her name was Emma Swallow, and Sousa soon proposed to her. But her father didn't approve. He said that because Sousa was a musician, he would almost certainly never make much money.

Sousa showed the same determination that he had some 15 years earlier when he stood outside in a rainstorm. He accepted a conducting position in Chicago he'd just been offered. Just before leaving, he went to Emma's father.

"I'll be gone for two years," he said. "I'm going to prove that I can make a good living. Then I'm coming back to marry Emma— no matter what you say."

His prediction was partly accurate. He was gone for two years. Though the Chicago job didn't last long, he soon found work with other groups. One was a traveling vaudeville show featuring nude girls in still poses representing famous paintings. They got into trouble in Pittsburgh where the girls were arrested. The band members barely avoided the same fate. Then in 1876, he got a steady job in Philadelphia.

When he saw Emma again the following year, her father approved of him and what he had done. But now there was a different problem. Another man also wanted to marry Emma. She hadn't told John Philip about him. He was so angry that he broke off the relationship and went back to Philadelphia.

He found work with music publishers in addition to his conducting and playing. He wrote an operetta, although it was never produced. And he became musical director of the new Amateur Opera Company. The company produced Gilbert and Sullivan's *H.M.S. Pinafore*, which had become extremely popular in the U.S. With Sousa's orchestration, *Pinafore* was very successful. Gilbert and Sullivan themselves saw a performance and liked it.

The *Pinafore* production also provided something far better than its creators' approval.

This is one of the many productions of Gilbert and Sullivan's HMS Pinafore. Sousa produced a version of the play when he became the musical director of the new Amateur Opera Company.

One of the young singers was Jane Bellis. When John Philip saw her early in 1879, it was love at first sight. According to his description in *Marching Along*, "She had a cloud of chestnut hair, and a perfect complexion. She was wearing a little gray poke bonnet and was charmingly dressed. I liked everything about her, her manner, her speech, her face, her voice." He liked her so well that they were married on December 30, 1879. He was 25 years old and she was 17. The Sousas would eventually have three children: John Philip, Jr., who was born in the spring of 1881, Jane Priscilla (1882) and Helen (1887).

Soon after the marriage, Sousa was asked to write the music for a variety show called *Our Flirtations,* which opened in Philadelphia and then went on tour. While in St. Louis, Sousa received exciting news: he was being considered to lead the Marine Band. After an exchange of telegrams, his father Antonio accepted the position by proxy.

During a rehearsal of HMS Pinafore, Sousa met his wife-to-be, Jane van Middlesworth Bellis, the daughter of a Philadelphia carpenter. Though her given name was Jane, John Philip always called her "Jennie." On Tuesday, December 30, 1879, John Philip and Jennie were married in a semi-private affair at her home. She was seventeen when they married and he was twenty-five. Here is a picture of the two of them years after their wedding.

So on October 1, 1880 John Philip Sousa again enlisted in the Marine Corps. But this time he wasn't a young apprentice. Now he was the leader of the Marine Band.

There was a certain grim satisfaction in taking over the position. He replaced Louis Schneider, who had humiliated him seven years earlier. In addition, he was the first American-born leader. He was conducting a military band for the first time. All of his professional experience had been as conductor of dance bands or theater orchestras.

That turned out to be a good thing.

He found the Marine Band in a sorry state. Because of his unique background, he approached the problems he faced quite differently than his predecessors.

One problem was that the collection of music was trite and old-fashioned. He set to work gathering the best works from Europe and America and writing new instrumentation. In the first year he added six new marches of his own.

The problems with the players were more serious. Their morale was poor. The pay was so low that they had to earn outside income with other musical engagements. Many of them wanted to leave the band but could not because their enlistment period was not over.

He also became much stricter with the band members. When Sousa began his appointment there were about 40 band members. In the first year the number dropped to nearly 30 as some of the poorer musicians couldn't keep up with the new leader's demands.

Before Sousa arrived most of the musicians had been Europeans. He replaced the ones who left with eager young Americans whom he recruited from among the players he had met in his travels. His younger brother George became a drummer in the band.

It didn't take long for the results to become apparent.

The band made its first appearance under Sousa's direction on New Year's Day, 1881 at a White House reception. Sousa knew that usual military band performances were too loud for a formal reception. So he played subdued music as ambassadors, cabinet members, and Supreme Court justices arrived. Then he picked up the tempo with lively polkas and marches when the general public arrived. The receiving line moved rapidly, tiring the outgoing president, Rutherford B. Hayes, less than usual.

The next president, James A. Garfield, was in office only briefly before he was killed by an assassin's bullet. The Marine Band did not even have an opportunity to play for him.

Garfield's vice-president, Chester A. Arthur, became the new president. But he was not familiar with military procedure. One day Sousa met the president's private secretary on the street. The secretary told him that the president wanted the band to play at the White House on the following Thursday. Sousa told the Marine Corps commandant, but by next Thursday he had received no orders to report to the White House. It was a fine mess. Friday morning he was called to report to the Secretary of the Navy. The president was upset because the Marine Band had not been at the White House the previous evening. It took a lot of talk and the help of a friendly congressman before the president's staff learned how to deal with military regulations.

Sousa later won President Arthur's approval. At a state dinner the president called the bandleader over and asked him to play the

Cachuca so a lady could do a Spanish dance to the tune. Sousa said that he didn't have the music with him but would include it on their next program. The president insisted, saying that he thought the Marine Band could play anything. Luckily one of the band members remembered the melody and played it softly for Sousa, who quickly wrote out parts for the major instruments. President Arthur was pleased.

Arthur's successor, Grover Cleveland, was the only president to be married in the White House. The Marine Band played all the music for the wedding. The distance from a room upstairs to the exact spot where the ceremony was to take place was carefully measured, and the Mendelssohn "Wedding March" was timed to the precise number of steps the wedding party would take. The band played the climax just as the bride and groom reached the clergyman.

After President Cleveland left office, Sousa and the Marine Band played for the official functions of President Benjamin Harrison. He was the fifth president Sousa had served.

Left, Chester A. Arthur and, right, Grover Cleveland. Sousa led the Marine Band during both Presidents' terms. His band even played at Grover Cleveland's wedding.

In spite of his demanding schedule as leader of the Marine Band, Sousa was also active as a composer. His marches were now being played by other bandmasters. He wrote a light opera, *The Smugglers*. It was not a success. Sousa spent exactly one night feeling bad about the failure. The next morning he started on a new opera, called *Desiree*. This one was popular and played for many weeks in Washington and Philadelphia.

The Marine Band's reputation improved dramatically and its concerts began to attract more sophisticated audiences. The band also became a snappy marching unit. A great part of the success came from Sousa's marches. In 1886 he composed "The Gladiator" and "The Rifle Regiment." Two years later he composed one of his most famous pieces, "Semper Fidelis." The title means "always faithful" and is the motto of the Marine Corps. It was eventually adopted as the official Marine anthem.

In 1889 the newspaper *Washington Post* asked Sousa to compose a march to promote an essay contest. The march, called "The Washington Post," was played on the grounds of the Smithsonian Institute when the contest winners were announced. The public loved it! It spread rapidly and was soon the number-one hit in both America and Europe. Dance masters used it for a new dance called the two-step.

At about this time, an article in a British band journal said that since Austrian composer Johann Strauss, Jr. was called the "Waltz King," John Philip Sousa should be called the "March King." Sousa's publisher saw the article and used the title to promote his music. Sousa has been known as the "March King" ever since then.

It wasn't a crown that Sousa wore lightly. Marches sound as if they are as easy to write as they are to listen to. Sousa knew that that wasn't true.

This is a picture of the U.S. Marine Band in Albany, New York in 1888. John Philip Sousa was the seventeenth leader of the Marine Band (three previous leaders had served twice) and the first American born. Under Sousa's leadership, the U.S. Marine Band reached the highest standard ever attained by an American military band.

"A march must be good," he wrote. "It must be as free from padding as a marble statue. Every line must be carved with unerring skill...There must be a melody which appeals to the musical and the unmusical alike."

Later in 1889 Sousa demonstrated his ability to win the hearts of his audiences. The band was ordered to play in Fayetteville, North Carolina. It was the 100th anniversary of North Carolina's ratification of the United States Constitution.

But the suffering of the Civil War years was still a very vivid memory in the South. Sousa could feel the discomfort and coolness of the audience as the band played "The Star Spangled Banner" and the state's governor gave a speech. He knew that they were expecting a concert of patriotic music—patriotic to the North, that is.

So Sousa said softly to his musicians, "Dixie." The band began playing that beloved song, and the crowd went wild. The cheering brought tears to Sousa's eyes. From then on he knew the value of playing what his audiences most wanted to hear.

It also let him know the value of touring. He wanted to show off his band to other parts of the country.

But he ran into a problem. ◆

This historic instrument was made for John Philip Sousa in 1893. The huge horn was made for use with Sousa's band at the original Chicago's World Fair, and was given by Sousa to Harry S. Hobson, musical composer at the exposition after the close of the fair. It has never been duplicated and is said to be a priceless relic of music history. This copper horn is an ancestor of the Sousaphone. It weighs 90 pounds and is just short of 6 feet in height.

RECONSTRUCTION

When the Civil War ended in 1865 the southern states were in ruins. Their young men were slaughtered, their plantations, public buildings, bridges, factories, and businesses destroyed. The states faced the task of rebuilding their governments and their society.

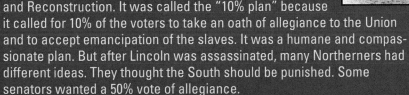

President Lincoln had foreseen the serious problems the reunited nation would face. In 1863, two years before the end of the war, he formulated a Proclamation of Amnesty and Reconstruction. It was called the "10% plan" because it called for 10% of the voters to take an oath of allegiance to the Union and to accept emancipation of the slaves. It was a humane and compassionate plan. But after Lincoln was assassinated, many Northerners had different ideas. They thought the South should be punished. Some senators wanted a 50% vote of allegiance.

There were others who wanted to make a profit from the calamity and misery. Radical Republican politicians wanted to maintain power by appealing to the southern black voters. Many Northerners went to the South to make money. They were called "carpetbaggers" because they carried all their possessions with them in cheap luggage made out of carpets. They took advantage of business and commercial opportunities.

In 1867 the United States Congress passed the Reconstruction Act. It divided the South into five military districts. Federal troops were sent to insure that the Southern population followed the new laws. But the Reconstruction policies did not change the social structures or the attitudes of the South. They only made a defeated people more angry and bitter.

Just as bad, political promises to the recently freed slaves were not kept. Many African Americans were more desperately poor than they had been as slaves. At least on the plantations they had food and shelter. Without education they faced a future of brutal poverty.

The Reconstruction period failed to solve the problems of Southern society. In fact, it caused additional bitterness and hatred. But there was one positive result. The 14th and 15th Amendments to the Constitution would be used a century later to protect minority rights during the Civil Rights era.

Shortly after Sousa married Jane Bellis in 1879, he grew his famous beard. As conductor of the U.S. Marine Band from 1880 to 1892, Sousa served under Presidents Hayes, Garfield, Cleveland, Arthur, and Harrison.

Masters of Music

CHAPTER 4

The Sousa Band

Despite the success of the trip to North Carolina, the Marine Corps commandant opposed Sousa's requests for a concert tour. The most he could get was a 24-hour furlough, which meant the band could only go as far as Baltimore or Philadelphia. When the commandant became seriously ill and was replaced, Sousa lost no time in asking permission to make a tour. He had to ask the Secretary of the Navy and President Harrison. Finally in 1891 he was able to arrange a five-week tour.

In his eagerness, Sousa scheduled two concerts a day in addition to luncheons, banquets, other public appearances and the constant travel. It was a great success with the public. Unfortunately the strain on his health caused him to collapse at the end of the tour. The Marine Corps surgeon sent the exhausted bandleader to Europe for a rest.

The trip wasn't much of a rest. The ship that the Sousas were aboard was in a terrible storm. Then it caught fire. They barely made it safely to England. Once in Europe the Sousas traveled to France and Germany.

As soon as he was back in Washington, Sousa began planning a second Marine Band tour. He had to talk fast to convince his superiors that he would be more careful of his health this time. Permission was granted. This second tour extended to the west coast and was even more popular than the first tour.

But its success was clouded near its conclusion. Sousa's father died on April 27, 1892.

Antonio had been proud of his son's success. If he'd lived another three days he would have been even prouder.

The man who organized the tours of the Marine Band was a professional concert manager named David Blakely. When the band arrived in Chicago on April 30, Blakely asked Sousa to think about resigning from the Marine Corps and organizing a civilian concert band. Blakely offered Sousa four times his Marine Corps salary plus a percentage of the profits. Sousa had always dreamed of having his own band. That way he wouldn't have to worry about getting permission to tour.

By the time the band got back to Washington, Sousa had made up his mind: he accepted Blakely's proposition. After twelve years of service for five presidents, John Philip Sousa requested his release from the Marine Corps.

On the first of August, 1892 Sousa left Washington for New York to begin organizing the Sousa Band. The first tour got off to a strong start. The band played at the World's Fair in Chicago and traveled eastward through New York.

Then trouble started. Blakely's inexperienced assistants had arranged part of the tour in New England. The bookings were in small towns and attendance at the concerts was poor. Blakely said that he was canceling the rest of the tour. Sousa was very angry. He insisted that the tour continue as scheduled. He would never go back on his word.

The tour continued, and business got better. It ended with a successful concert in New York. Sousa learned an important lesson from the near disaster. After that he distrusted managers and paid close attention to business dealings. Not long afterward, he ended his dealings with the Coleman music publishing company. They had purchased Sousa's marches for $35 each, without any royalty payments. Sousa's music had made Coleman a very wealthy man. Sousa contracted a much better deal with the John Church Company of Cincinnati. This time he would get royalties. The first of his marches published by Church was "The Liberty Bell." With the royalty arrangement, that march alone earned him over $40,000 in less than seven years.

The success of the Sousa Band after that first difficult tour was amazing. John Philip Sousa played what audiences wanted to hear. He gathered the best musicians he could find, and he trained and rehearsed them. He paid them well and treated them with respect. The band became like a very large, happy, traveling family.

In the beginning, many of the musicians were European. Before many years had passed, they were all American born except one, and he was a naturalized citizen. Sousa and his musicians, like most Americans, loved sports. The band had its own baseball and basketball teams.

As a talented and disciplined organization governed by mutual respect, the Sousa Band was equal to whatever situations it encountered. One night in St. Louis, an enormous throng packed the huge music hall. Suddenly the lights went out. In the complete darkness, Sousa could tell by sharp cries and sounds of feet that the audience was about to panic. If hundreds of frightened people began stampeding toward the exits, many could be killed or seriously injured.

He called softly, "Yankee Doodle." His musicians responded instantly, playing the song from memory in the dark. They quickly followed with "Dixie" and a popular tune called "Oh Dear, What Can the Matter Be?" By that time the audience was relaxed and laughing. The band kept playing familiar songs until the lights came back on and the scheduled concert program continued.

In its thirty-nine years, the Sousa Band visited every part of the United States and Canada, made four tours of Europe and one world tour. They traveled 1,200,000 miles. It became the most famous musical organization in the world. All the expenses were paid for by their drawing power in attracting enthusiastic audiences. The programs were designed to please the listeners—Sousa played everything from the works of classical European composers to ragtime and jazz. Of course the programs always included his own marches. Surprisingly, though, despite Sousa's reputation as the "March King," his band was a concert band. It marched just seven times during its existence.

In his autobiography, Sousa wrote about his relationship to his musicians. He said, "The leader who doesn't watch for outbursts of genius in his men, in the playing of a phrase, makes a sad mistake." He went on to explain that he would listen, during break periods, to the men practicing their parts different ways. When he heard an interpretation he liked, he would introduce it to the band, saying, "His way is better than mine." In this way the music of the Sousa band stayed very much alive and improved from one year to the next.◆

THE PHONOGRAPH FYInfo

The word "phonograph" comes from two Greek words, *phono*, meaning "sound" and *graphos*, meaning "writing."

In France in 1855, Leon Scott de Martinville invented the first successful device for recording sound. Called a "phonauto-graph," it used a mouthpiece with a membrane that was attached to a stylus. The stylus recorded sound waves on a cylinder covered with carbon-covered paper. The sounds could not be played back, but this first effort to record them was the foundation of later devices.

Twenty years later, Thomas Edison designed the "tinfoil phonograph." This was a cylindrical drum wrapped in tinfoil. The mouthpiece and diaphragm were connected to a stylus that etched sound patterns on the rotating foil. To play back the sound, a more sensitive vibrating "repro-ducer" replaced the mouthpiece. Edison recited "Mary Had a Little Lamb" for the first demonstration. Even though he expected success, he was surprised to hear his own voice. In 1878 investors created the Edison Speaking Phonograph Company to manufacture and exhibit the talking machines. But Edison quickly lost interest as he moved on to his next great invention, the electric light.

Nearly a decade later, Alexander Graham Bell, who had invented the telephone in 1876, improved the phonograph. The main improvement was making the cylinder out of wax instead of cardboard and tinfoil. This allowed for longer and clearer recordings.

The competition from Bell motivated Edison to renew interest in his phonograph. He also used wax on the cylinders. He wanted the device to be practical. So he marketed it as an office dictation machine. But it never really caught on among the nation's businessmen and secretaries.

However, an entirely new use emerged: playing music. By 1890 a commercial recording industry began. Musicians would record on several phonographs at once. They repeated their performances until they made enough cylinders to sell. In drugstores and cafes, coin-operated phonographs played two minutes of music for a nickel. The music that recorded best on the early wax cylinders had a strong rhythm and melody, such as waltzes, polkas, and marches.

The result was that as the 20th Century began, phonographs became the first form of mass media entertainment, before radio, movies, and television.

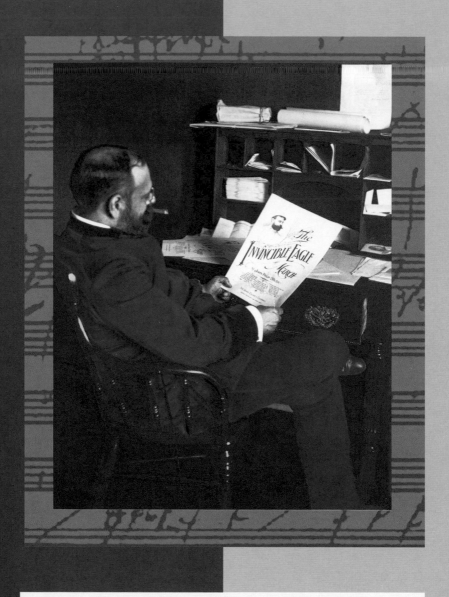

John Philip Sousa has always been, and continues to be the band composer most often recorded. Several American bands kept the Sousa tradition alive for years, not the least of which is the U.S. Marine Band. Most Marine Band concerts include at least one selection of their former band leader. On October 7, 1974, the concert hall at the Marine Barracks in Washington was formally designated the John Philip Sousa Band Hall.

CHAPTER 5

Patriot

John Philip Sousa's era—the years between the Civil War and the Great Depression—was a time of growth and progress, of optimism and patriotism. He and his music became symbolic of that period in this nation's history.

Like many other Americans, Sousa believed in the value of hard work. He was not satisfied with having the most popular and successful touring band in the country. By 1895 he was the undisputed "March King." The marches he composed were heard everywhere, not only at band concerts but also in ballrooms. But there was another musical form that John Philip Sousa wanted to conquer: the operetta.

Eleven years earlier, a singer named De Wolf Hopper had made his first appearance in Sousa's comic opera *Desiree*. Hopper now had his own company and wanted Sousa to write the music for an operetta called *El Capitan*. Sousa read the libretto—the story—and liked it. He completed the musical score in the summer of 1895. The show was an overwhelming success.

The following year, Sousa and his wife left for a vacation in Europe. But he soon lear ned that David Blakely, the band's manager, had died suddenly. With the band scheduled for another long tour, Sousa had to return at once to handle all the details.

"Here came one of the most vivid incidents of my career," he wrote in *Marching Along*. "As the vessel (the *Teutonic*) steamed out of the harbor I was pacing on the deck, absorbed in thoughts of my manager's death and the many duties and decisions which awaited me in New York. Suddenly, I began to sense a rhythmic beat of a band playing within my brain. Throughout the whole tense voyage, that imaginary band continued to unfold the same themes, echoing and re-echoing the most distinct melody. I did not transfer a note of that music to paper while I was on the steamer, but when we reached shore, I set down the measures that my brain-band had been playing for me, and not a note of it has ever changed."

Ever since then, thousands of real-life bands have played the march that Sousa's "brain-band" first played in 1896.

It is "The Stars and Stripes Forever."

It is probably the most famous composition by an American. It was included in every concert that the Sousa Band performed. In 1987, "The Stars and Stripes Forever" was officially declared the national march of the United States.

When the Spanish-American War began in 1898, Sousa composed a patriotic pageant called *The Trooping of the Colors*. He tried to re-enlist in the Marines, but found no suitable position available. He then volunteered for the Army with the condition that he be allowed to complete the tours for which he was committed. At the end of his 1898 tour, however, he fell seriously ill with typhoid fever and pneumonia for twelve weeks. By the time he recovered the war was over.

In 1900 the Sousa Band took American music to Europe. One reason for their European tour was to celebrate the independence of both France and America at the Paris Exposition. They played 175 concerts in 34 European cities.

The band had a very creative publicity man named George Hinton who traveled ahead to promote interest in the performances. His job had been easy in the United States where everyone knew about the Sousa Band. But it was unknown in Europe. So Hinton came up with a story to create interest. In Germany he spread the rumor that Sousa was actually a German immigrant named Siegfried Ochs, whose luggage had been labeled S.O., U.S.A. In France the supposed immigrant became S. Oulette. In England he was Sam Ogden.

To the tune of "The Stars and Stripes Forever," fireworks explode over the Hollywood Bowl during the 2002 edition of the July Fourth Spectacular in Los Angeles, California.

The problem with this story was that people liked it so much it wouldn't die. No matter how much Sousa insisted that he was an American named Sousa, his European audiences liked the idea that he was actually one of their countrymen. They loved the music and wanted to believe one of their own had created it. Soon the story took on a life of its own and cropped up in all the countries the band visited.

Back in the United States, Sousa and other composers were concerned about a new invention: the phonograph. This device was making Sousa's music more popular than ever before as recordings of his marches reached an even larger audience. But Sousa was afraid that it would win audiences away from live performances. In 1906 he wrote an article titled "The Menace of Mechanical Music" in which he blasted the recording industry.

John Philip Sousa and Victor Herbert, a very successful composer of light opera, testified before Congress at hearings for a new copyright law that would allow royalties on recorded music as well as printed music. After the bill was passed in 1907, Herbert and Sousa became officers in the newly formed Authors' and Composers' Copyright League of America. After winning these victories, Sousa felt much more positive about "mechanical music."

In 1910 the Sousa Band began a world tour, its most extensive trip. In addition to appearing in Europe they traveled to South Africa, Australia and New Zealand, Fiji Islands and Hawaii. Finally the band returned to the west coast and ended with a tour across the U.S. After this tour, Sousa relaxed with his favorite sport of trapshooting.

He was one of the best trap shooters in the country. Although he was also an excellent hunter, he preferred shooting clay targets, called "pigeons," in trapshooting meets. An English minister read that Sousa had shot a large number of "pigeons" and wrote to the composer, urging him to stop this murderous practice. Sousa replied by sending the minister a box of broken clay targets along with a note suggesting that they be broiled before eating.

By this time, Sousa and his family had been living in hotels in New York City for more than two decades. He had long since become a millionaire, so he bought a mansion on Long Island. Called "Wildbank," it would be his home for the rest of his life.

The Sousa Band was regrouped after World War I. Changing times brought some changes in the band's format, but the programs continued in the usual tradition. Here is the band at the Steel Pier in Atlantic City in 1929.

Three years later America declared war on Germany, entering World War I. John Philip Sousa accepted a commission in the United States Navy to train young bandsmen. He was 62 years old—the oldest man to enlist in the navy up until that time. At his request, he was paid the salary of exactly one dollar a month. He took his best musicians on tour to promote Liberty Bond sales. Despite his age, he marched every step of the way leading the huge 300-piece Navy Marching Band in parades.

Many expected Sousa to retire after World War I was over. He didn't. He regrouped the Sousa Band and continued. Most other touring bands went out of business in the 1920's, but Sousa continued to understand what the audiences wanted. Although he wasn't particularly fond of jazz himself, he included some jazz works in his programs along with his famous marches.

John Philip Sousa said that he would never retire, never give a farewell performance. He never did. In February of 1932 he conducted the bands of the Army, Navy, and Marines in front of the Capitol building in Washington as part of the 200th anniversary celebration of George Washington's birth. A few days later he conducted the U.S. Marine Band in what turned out to be his final concert.

Early in March he traveled to Reading, Pennsylvania where he was to direct the Ringgold Band in a concert. He registered in his hotel and then went to the American Legion hall to rehearse with the band. The last work he directed was "The Stars and Stripes Forever."

At a banquet that evening he gave a short speech, signed autographs, and returned to his hotel. At 1:30 the following morning—Sunday, March 6, 1932—John Philip Sousa died of a heart attack.

The man was dead, but his music will live as long as there are bands and parades and celebrations. ◆

Trapshooting

Trapshooting is sometimes called the "hidden sport." Millions of people enjoy it. Thousands of competitions are held every year. The world's best trapshooters compete every four years in the Olympic Games. Yet many people do not even know about this sport.

Trapshooting started to give hunters shooting practice so they would be more skilled when hunting ducks, pheasants, and other game birds. Soon, however, it became a separate sport.

The first trapshooting contest was held at the Sportsmen's Club of Cincinnati, Ohio in 1831. Live pigeons or sparrows were probably the targets. In 1866 glass ball targets were introduced. Glass ball shooters like Doc Carver and Annie Oakley set records in exhibitions and matches. The first clay target, invented by George Ligowsky, was introduced in 1880 and became an instant success. Known as a "clay pigeon," it is a saucer-sized disk.

Shooters stand at least 16 yards behind a trap concealed in an underground bunker. The trap is a spring device designed to throw the targets into the air at different angles. The shooter doesn't know from which direction the target will suddenly emerge, just as hunters don't know where birds will fly. The object is to hit the target by shooting it with a shotgun.

The first trapshooting organizations were for professional shooters who competed for money or gave exhibitions sponsored by gun or ammunition companies. Soon more and more amateur shooters became interested in the sport. The American Amateur Trapshooting Association, the first trapshooting organization entirely run by amateurs, was formed in 1915. Sousa was its first president.

Now the ATA (Amateur Trapshooting Association) has over 54,000 members. Its headquarters are in Vandalia, Ohio. Every August the Grand American World Trapshooting Championships are held there. About 6,000 shooters compete in three events over a 10-day period: singles (one target is released at a time), doubles (two targets are thrown at the same time and both must be hit), and the handicap event (the most difficult). In the handicap shooters are assigned a distance from the trap on the basis of their past performances. The most skilled shooters are placed 27 yards back. Only twice in the last ten years has a Grand American Handicap champion shot from the 27-yard line.

Selected Works

Marches

Sousa composed 136 marches. The most famous:
"Bonnie Annie Laurie"
"El Capitan"
"The Gladiator"
"The High School Cadets"
"King Cotton"
"The Liberty Bell"
"The Rifle Regiment"
"Semper Fidelis" (official march of the United
    States Marine Corps)
"The Stars and Stripes Forever" (official march of
    the United States of America)
"The Washington Post"

Operettas

Of Sousa's 15 operettas, the most successful were:
    El Capitan and *Desiree*

Songs

Most of Sousa's 70 songs set the words of well-
    known poems to music. These include
    "Boots" by Rudyard Kipling," "In
    Flanders Fields the Poppies Grow" by
    John D. McCrae and "Crossing the Bar"
    by Alfred Lord Tennyson.

Waltzes and other dances

Among Sousa's 24 dances, the most popular
    waltzes are "The Colonial Dames
    Waltzes" and "The Lady of the White
    House." Of his other dances the
    "Presidential Polonaise" is the best
    known.

Humoresques

These 14 instrumental pieces included "Among My
    Souvenirs," "A Little Peach in the
    Orchard Grew," "Look for the Silver
    Lining," "Showing Off Before Com-
    pany" and "Swanee."

Chronology

1854	born on November 6 in Washington, DC
1868	enlists in Marine Corps to play in Marine Band
1872	publishes first composition, "Moonlight on the Potomac Waltzes"
1875	leaves Marine Corps
1876	goes to Philadelphia to work as a professional musician
1879	marries Jane Bellis
1880	becomes leader of the Marine Band
1881	birth of son, John Philip Sousa, Jr.
1882	birth of daughter, Jane Priscilla Sousa
1887	birth of daughter, Helen Sousa
1892	starts Sousa Band; death of father, Antonio Sousa
1896	composes "The Stars and Stripes Forever"
1900	Sousa Band tours Europe
1901	second European tour
1903	third European tour
1904	fourth European tour
1906	With fellow composer Victor Herbert, testifies in favor of giving composers royalty payments for recorded music
1907	becomes treasurer of newly formed Authors' and Composers' Copyright League of America
1910	tours around the world with the Sousa Band
1914	purchases home on Long Island called "Wildbank"
1917	joins Naval Reserves and becomes leader of the U.S. Navy Marching Band
1932	dies in Reading, Pennsylvania

Timeline in History

1849	California Gold Rush begins
1860	Abraham Lincoln elected president
1861	Civil War begins
1863	Emancipation Proclamation frees slaves in Confederate states
1865	Lee surrenders to Grant at Appomattox to end Civil War; President Lincoln assassinated
1868	Ulysses S. Grant elected president
1871	Great Chicago fire destroys city
1876	Alexander Graham Bell invents telephone; Rutherford Hayes elected president
1880	James A. Garfield elected president
1881	Chester A. Arthur becomes president after Garfield is assassinated
1884	Grover Cleveland elected president
1886	Statue of Liberty dedicated in New York Harbor
1893	World's Fair opens in Chicago
1897	Klondike gold rush in Alaska begins
1898	Sinking of battleship *Maine* in Havana harbor begins Spanish-American War
1901	President McKinley assassinated; Theodore Roosevelt becomes president
1903	Wright brothers fly first successful airplane at Kitty Hawk
1906	San Francisco earthquake and fire destroy city
1908	Henry Ford introduces the Model T
1912	Luxury liner *Titanic* sinks after striking iceberg
1914	Panama Canal opens; World War I begins in Europe
1917	United States declares war on Germany
1918	Germany signs armistice treaty ending World War I
1920	18th Amendment begins Prohibition; 19th Amendment provides women with right to vote
1925	John T. Scopes prosecuted for teaching Darwin's theory of evolution
1927	Charles Lindbergh makes first solo transatlantic flight from New York to Paris; first talking motion picture, *The Jazz Singer*
1928	Herbert Hoover elected president
1929	Great Depression begins with stock market crash
1931	Empire State Building opens in New York City
1932	Franklin D. Roosevelt elected president
1987	*Stars and Stripes Forever* legislated as the official march of the U.S.

Further Reading

For Young Adult Readers:
Greene, Carol. *John Philip Sousa: The March King.* Chicago: Children's Press, 1992.
Lutz, Norma Jean. *Marching with Sousa.* Westwood, NJ: Barbour & Co., 1998.

Works Consulted:
Berger, Kenneth. *The March King and His Band.* New York: Exposition Press, 1957.
Bierley, Paul E. *John Philip Sousa: American Phenomenon.* Westerville, Ohio: Integrity Press, 1973.
Bierley, Paul E. *The New Grove Dictionary of Music and Musicians.* London: Macmillan, 1980.
Bierley, Paul E. *The Works of John Philip Sousa.* Westerville, Ohio: Integrity Press, 1984.
Lingg, Ann M. *John Philip Sousa.* New York: Henry Holt and Co., 1954.
Sousa, John Philip. *Marching Along.* Westerville, Ohio: Integrity Press, 1994.

On the Internet:
Who Was John Philip Sousa?
http://www.pbs.org/thinktank/show_903.html

John Philip Sousa, American Composer, Conductor, & Patriot
http://www.dws.org/sousa/

John Philip Sousa: Library of Congress article
http://www.loc.gov/rr/hispanic/portam/sousa.html

"The President's Own" United States Marine Band: John Philip Sousa
http://www.marineband.usmc.mil/edu_sousa.html

Historical Footnote:
John Philip Sousa's "The Stars and Stripes Forever" was legislated the national march of the United States of America after ten bills introduced in Congress all failed. A concentrated effort was made in 1986 and petitions were circulated. Finally, the bill passed in both houses of Congress, and it was signed by then-President Reagan on December 11, 1987.

Of all the memorials and tributes that have given legendary status to John Philip Sousa, the activities of the Sousa Band Fraternal Society were unique in the years after Sousa's death. They held annual meetings in his honor until the late 1980s, when only 22 members of the Sousa Band Fraternal Society were still alive. It is likely that few, if any are still alive as this book goes to press (2003).

The Detroit Concert Band is one civilian band that has kept Sousa's memory alive. The band recorded all of Sousa's published works in a series of ten recordings known as the *Sousa American Bicentennial Collection.*

Glossary

apprentice (uh-PREN-tus) - someone learning a craft or trade from an employer

autobiography (aw-toh-bye-OG-ruff-ee) - written story of one's own life

commandant (CAW-man-dahnt) - commanding officer in the military services

conservatory (kun-SURV-uh-tor-ee) - school of music or art

harmony (HAR-mun-ee) - relationship between two or more musical notes played or sung at the same time

immigrant (IM-uh-grent) - someone who enters a country to live in it

instrumentation (in-struh-men-TAY-shun) - arrangement of a piece of music for particular instruments

libretto (lib-RET-oh) - words of an opera, operetta or other piece of vocal music

operetta (aw-puh-RET-uh) - short, light opera, usually with spoken dialogue

optimism (OP-tuh-mizm) - belief that everything will be for the best

orchestrate (OR-kuh-strayt) - arrange music for performance by a band or orchestra

perfect pitch (PUR-fekt PITCH) - ability to recognize or produce any musical note

pneumonia (new-MOAN-ya) - dangerous disease of the lungs

proxy (PROK-see) - authority given by one person for another to act on his or her behalf

reception (ree-SEP-shun) - formal social gathering where guests are greeted individually

royalty (ROY-ul-tee) - percentage of money received in sales by the owner of a copyright to a work of art

trite (TRITE) - boring because of too much repetition

Index